PRAISE FOR THE TEDACABIN

"So far I am happy because there's a lot of improvement. I hope we can continue to make good decisions"-Cameo Hlongwane (Marine Engineer)

"You are Prince of Africa. Your educational trading content is good and I trust your analyses-Badal Liban Mahamod- Medical Student

"I will trade with you for the rest of my life, you are my Forex teacher"- Hussein Haji Adan – Student from Somalia

PRICE ACTION

THE ULTIMATE INDICATOR

Take immediate control of your financial destiny.

Trade the Forex Market with a deadly accurate Price Action strategy.

FILLEMON HELONDO

THE TEDACABIN

INTRODUCTION

In a nutshell, FOREX trading is the speculation on strength or weakness of particular currencies throughout the world and then taking a decision to buy or sell.

If I were to analyse that the New Zealand Dollar (NZD) was going to strengthen over the next few hours and the American Dollar (USD) was going to weaken over the next few hours, I would buy the NZDUSD currency pair which means that I am buying NZD vs. USD because I believe the NZD will be stronger in due course and I can then sell it for a profit.

Now there is obviously allot more to it than this but that should give you a basic understanding of what FOREX trading consists of.

Looking at the EURAUD chart below. Only 6 scaled trades, 0.6 Standard Lot total risk and over 2000 pips in profits when I got out. All these in just 12 days.

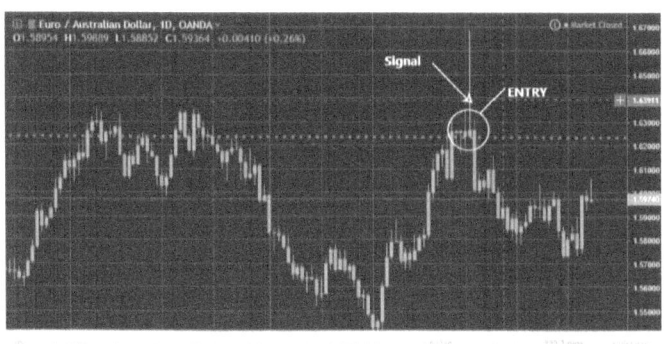

Sniper Shot Accuracy! Price Action signal was spotted on the daily chart and the entry was taken on the following day open.

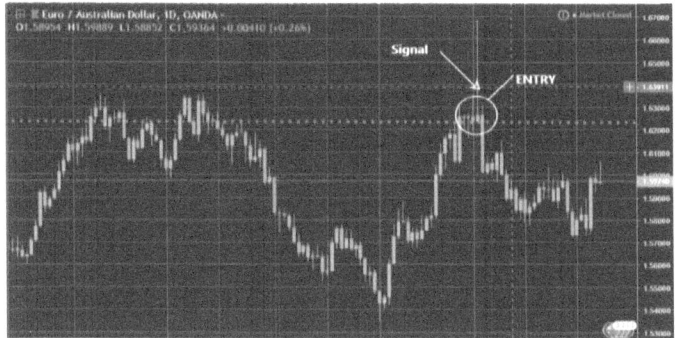

Just less than 12 hours in the trade and already 200 pips reached. This is the power of the Sniper entry Price Action Trading Strategy.

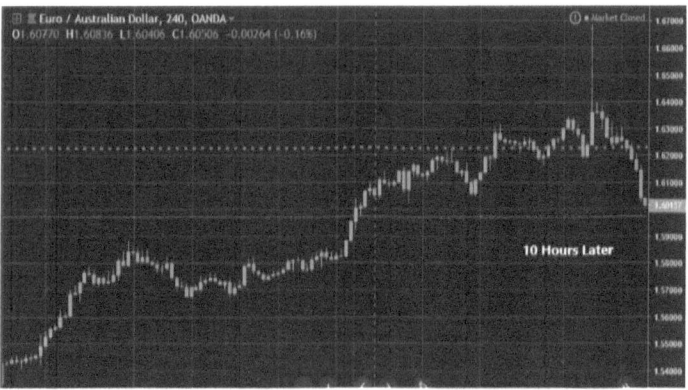

Price Action Trading:

- Is Simple to apply
- Helps you to take Sniper shot accurate trades and allow you to catch massive pip moves effortlessly.
- Encourages the set and forget trading style which reduces your chart time, if you have other obligations such as work.
- Adopts the contrarian trader style which is a highly successful trading approach.

PRICE ACTION TRADING OVERVIEW

Timeframe: Daily

Currency Pair: Any

Indicators: None

Below is a General setup for a buy trade:

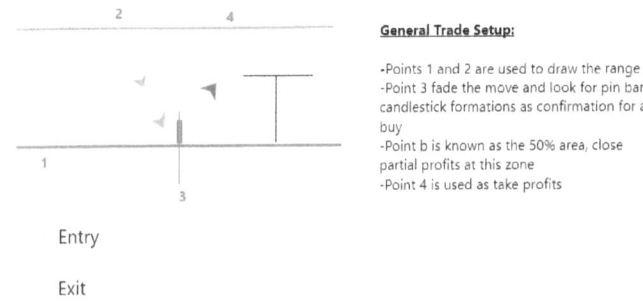

General Trade Setup:

-Points 1 and 2 are used to draw the range
-Point 3 fade the move and look for pin bar candlestick formations as confirmation for a buy
-Point b is known as the 50% area, close partial profits at this zone
-Point 4 is used as take profits

Entry

Exit

Below is a General setup for a sell trade:

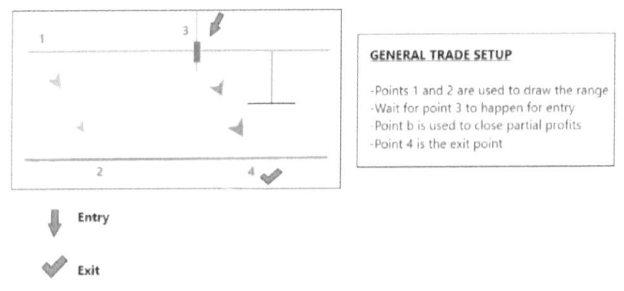

GENERAL TRADE SETUP

-Points 1 and 2 are used to draw the range
-Wait for point 3 to happen for entry
-Point b is used to close partial profits
-Point 4 is the exit point

Entry

Exit

Notice how the Pin Bar formation is easy to spot and trade:

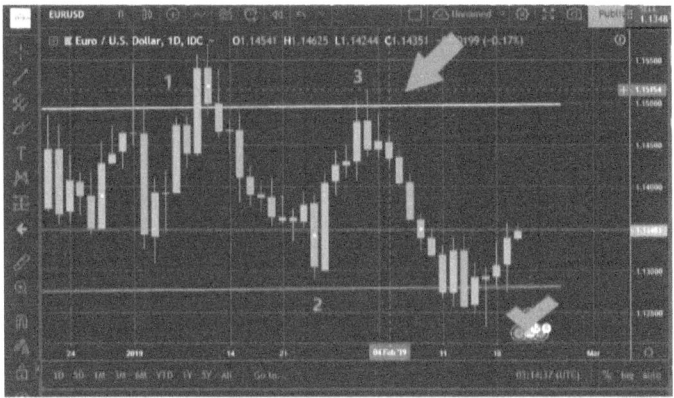

I want you to identify the Inside Pin Bar formation and how price reacted after this setup. Price moved a total of 200 points making this a clear sniper shot entry. You need to understand that PRICE Action is the ULTIMATE INDICATOR. Everything you need to know in order to place a trade all lies within the price action itself. Indicators are just fancy lagging gadgets applied by traders who refuse to keep it simple.

Let's look at one more chart.

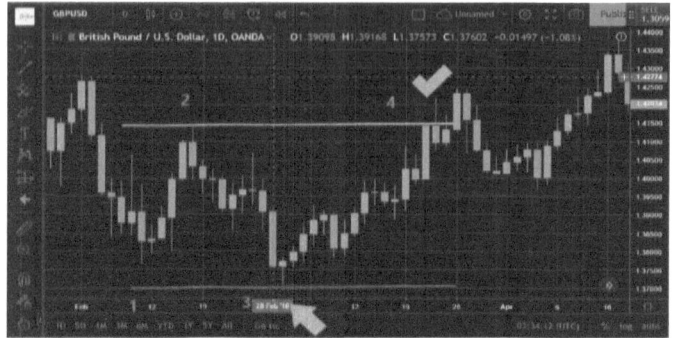

Notice the Pin Bar Formation at 3? Would you have made money if you took this trade? Yes. Simplicity Pays!

When trading with price action you need to have a good understanding of candlestick formations. There are a lot of formations out there and different ways on how to trade them. But by learning how to identify the types of pin bars and how to trade them which I will show you, then that's all you will need to know to trade price action successfully.

You need to build a good understanding of pin bar formations.

This includes:

- How to identify different types of Pin Bars
- How to trade Pin Bars
- Where to Place your stop and profit target
- Applying confluence or supporting factors to trade Pin Bars
- Understand Technical Analysis

Understanding the points above will allow you to trade much like a contrarian trader. Placing Sniper Shot Accurate Entries.

UNDERSTANDING PIN BARS:

These are one the most important formations on a price chart. Pin bars are what I look for when I analyse the charts and today you will learn how to identify them and what they mean.

❖ **A PIN BAR CANDLESTICK HAS A NOTICEABLY LONGER TAIL THAN THE BODY (AREA BETWEEN THE OPEN AND CLOSE PRICE)**

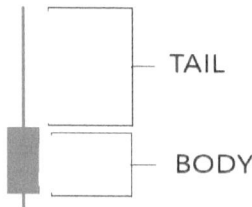

A tail on a bar indicates that price MIGHT move in the opposite direction. This a very important piece of price formation for a price action trader. Pin Bars that form on the daily chart carry more weight and they are the most important.

You can entirely base your trading around these price action formations and timeframe only.

Pin Bar formations are your channel to the gold mine. You have got to love them, understand them and trade them with confidence when they appear on the daily charts. See below how powerful the implication of a Pin Bar formations has to the overall directional trend. You can catch amazing market moves by having the patience to wait for your trades to play out and by understanding how to identify and trade Pin Bar Formations.

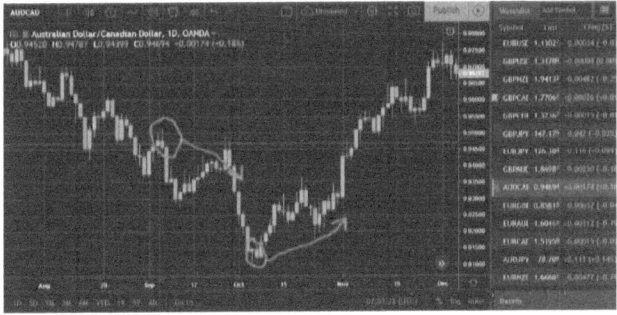

Let's take a look again at the GBPUSD currency pair below and see how pin bar formations may have given confirmation to take trades promising massive moves:

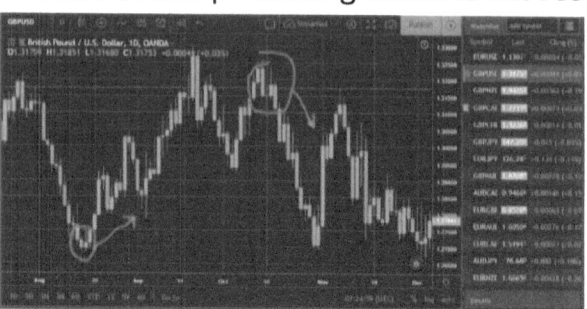

Why trade with Pin Bars?

Pin Bar candlesticks indicates a rejection of a level or price area and either a small, medium or large reversal that happened quite quickly. Pin Bars indicate to us that there was exhaustion at that area the tail formed, which has powerful implications. When we identify an area price is becoming exhausted at, it means there is something happening that we need to take note of.

That tail is showing us that either buyers really wanted to buy there, or sellers really wanted to sell, why? Doesn't really matter.

Look at the USDZAR chart below, see all the red circles where I circled the Pin Bars and the implications they had on Price Action. You can easily identify the exhaustion at this circled areas and how the reversals happened quite evidently after the Pin Bar Formations.

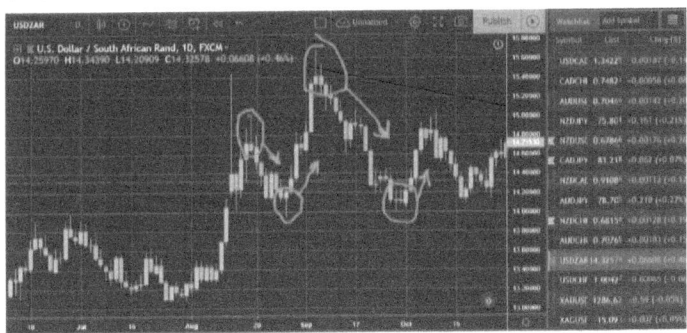

Before I show you how to trade the Pin Bar formation, you will need to understand the different types of Pin Bars, their general formations and what their implications are to the overall price direction.

Now, let's get started in learning about some of the best Pin Bar candlestick formations...

2 TYPES OF TAILED PIN BAR FORMATIONS:

a) Pin Bar Candlestick

The Pin Bar has a longer tail than the body, the body is the distance between the open and close. The tail on a pin bar should be at least 2/3 the length of the total bar. Sometimes, there is little or no body. The implication is that price may move the other direction, opposite the tail. See examples of a Pin Bar on the following page...

Bullish Pin Bar (Buy Signal

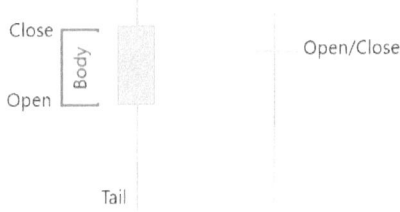

Bearish Pin Bar (Sell Signal)

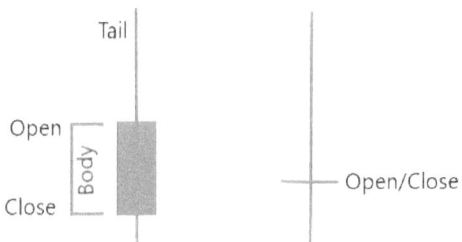

Remember this chart? You could have taken these trades with almost pin-point accuracy and there is no way you could've missed these trades. We are looking at the daily chart here not the noisy 1 hour or 30 minute charts.

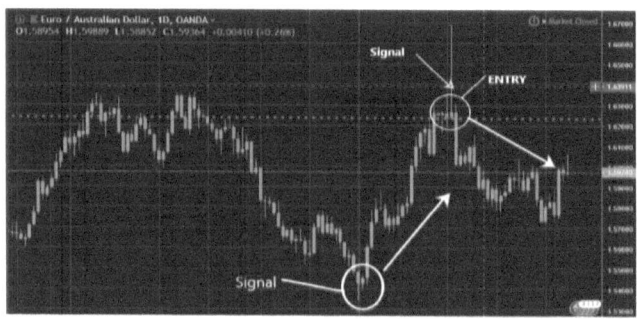

b) Double Pin Bar Candlestick Formation

These type of Pin Bar formation consists of two consecutive Pin Bar formations. These formations are common and most like to appear at resistance or support zones. They are strong indication that price is most likely to surge in the opposite direction.

Let's take a look at an example of a Double Pin Bar formation below…

Bullish Double Pin Bar (Buy Signal

Bearish Double Pin Bar (Sell Signal)

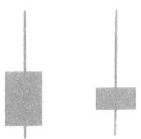

See the NZDUSD chart below, notice how massive these surges in Price Action are? This is the power of Pin Bar Formations… You don't need fancy indicators and what not's… No! Just pure price action.

I noticed that there are some candlestick formations on the 4 hour chart and weekly charts. Is it okay to trade Pin Bar formations on any other chart than the daily chart

The H4 Pin Bar shows a reversal in price across the 4 hour period, whereas the daily chart pin bar shows a reversal in price across that day's period. The higher the timeframe the more powerful the signal.

**Q**UESTION

Do you only use Pin Bars to trade the market? Or are there other technical analytic skills I will need to trade Pin Bars successfully?

ANSWER   **Trading Pin Bars with confluence will have all odds stacked in your favour. Therefore understanding the chart context will allow you to filter the signals in different market conditions. Effectively, I will teach you how to apply supporting factors to trade pin bars which is the key element in profitable trading.**

UNDERSTANDING SUPPORT AND RESISTANCE:

Markets do not move in a straight line, they go up, they come down and they move sideways. As they make peaks and troughs we call these turning points/zones Support and Resistance levels.

Support and Resistance levels are the main elements of technical analysis and they help us build a component which helps us understand the market environment. With clearly outlined support and resistance levels we can make sense of the market condition in terms of what it has done, what it is doing and how we may anticipate its next move.

Support and Resistance levels can be used to find high probability trades in range bound markets, determine trends and define risk vs. reward targets.

Note: Support and Resistance areas combined with Pin Bar pattern formation can be used as confluence to place a trade. Pin Bars that occur at support levels carry more weight as a buying signals and Pin Bar forming at resistance levels carry more weight as sell signals giving a price action trader an opportunity to trade the common fake breakout setups.

I will explain in detail, the different types of support and resistance levels, how to draw them and how you can use them as supporting factor when trading pin bar formations.

3 Types of Support and Resistance levels:

a. **Ranging Support and Resistance levels**
In a range bound market price action bounces between two parallel levels finding support and resistance at the lower and upper levels respectively. Range bound markets provide high probability trading opportunities for the price action trader.

The key is to first identify a ranging market, which is basically price bouncing between two parallel levels and look for trade entries at those levels. So if the trade is moving up towards the upper resistance level look to trade the opposite way i.e. sell rather than anticipating a breakout. Or look to buy when price is approaching the lower support level.

You can literally do this until price finally breaks outside of these range to find newer highs or lows. Let's take a look at real life example of a Ranging Support and Resistance levels in the market.

Do you understand what I am showing you here? Notice the circled pin Bars forming near the parallel levels and how easy they are to trade. Indeed, Price Action is THE ULTIMATE INDICATOR!

b. Swing Point Support and Resistance levels in trends

Support and Resistance levels are interchangeable, old support becomes resistance once broken an old resistance becomes support. This phenomenon can be confirmed in an upwards or downwards trending market when the market makes higher highs and higher lows or lower lows and lower highs. Swing point levels can then be marked as support or resistance as they form. We can then look to trade on retracements when Pin Bars form at these swing points.

Swing Point levels are great points to find entries into the market and can also be used to define risk and target levels by placing stop losses behind these levels.

The Gold/XAUUSD chart above shows a clear example of swing point support and resistance levels. On the left side of the chart you can find sell trades as the market retraces to the previous resistance level. Or Find Buy entries on the right hand side of the chart when price retraces back to support.

c) 50% Retracement Support and Resistance Levels

Easily calculated with Fibonacci retracement tool, it is a well-known phenomenon that the market always holds the half-way point of the swing, where market retraces before continuing with the overall trend or original move.

Can you see why support and resistance levels are important to the price action trader?

- Start paying close attention at identifying these levels on your charts.
- And also pay careful attention to the types of candlestick forming near these levels. Which type of candlesticks are we looking to trade once again? Yes, that's right Pin Bars only.

COMBINING SUPPORT AND RESISTANCE FOR TRADE SETUPS:

Placing trades with enough supporting factor is one powerful technique that will help you get into high probability trade setups and it is to your great advantage to be able to spot these setups.

Look at the chart on the following page:

With clearly defined ranging support and resistance levels on this chart you can use these levels as supporting factor to enter a trade when the pin bar patterns form.

Looking at the left hand side of the chart notice how the resistance level turned into a support level giving the price action trader an opportunity for a buy trade setup.

Observe the charts below. What can you say about the candlesticks that has just formed after the formation of the pin bar?

Chart 1: Bullish Pin Bar

The charts below are an example of
Bearish Pin Bar setup:

Assuming that you have confirmation of
the overall trend and have clear defined
support and resistance levels. At what
point would you have placed your entries
and where would you place your stop
loss if you were to trade the above pin
bars that have just formed on the daily
charts?

Let's take a look at the basic characteristics of candlesticks and how to trade these powerful setups…A candlestick has four distinctive features. Its open, high, low and close price.

Bearish Pin Bar

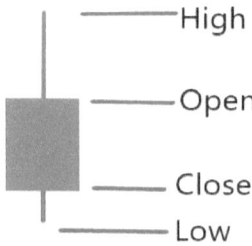

High
Open
Close
Low

Bullish Pin Bar

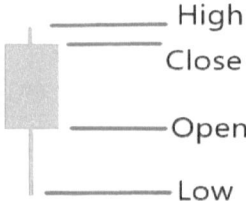

High
Close
Open
Low

Now take a look at the full chart below so that you get a bigger picture of the trade setups I showed you earlier.

If you take a closer look at the zoomed in charts on the previous page, you will notice that price smoothly reacted to the pin bar formations. Is this always the case? Most of the times this is a normal occurrence. In some occurrences you will find that price will form multiple pin bars (Double Pin Bar formations) before actually moving off in the anticipated direction from its exhaustion area.

It is very important to remain patient while trading pin bars and allow your trade to play out without interfering by making impulsive decisions. These trade setups took an average of 7 days each to play out fully with massive pip gains. So you too can tell the importance patience in this regard in order to catch these massive moves in the market.

Why are the Pin Bars that have formed on the daily chart considered more significant than the Pin Bars forming on a lower timeframe?

Pin Bar patterns occurring on lower timeframes indicate short term exhaustion in price action. These may have short term implications on price action. However, pin bars patterns on the daily chart will have Long term implications on price action which can last for several days or even weeks.

We can further classify Pin Bar Implications into 3 types:

- **Short term Pin Bars**
  Forming on chart timeframes between 1min and 30 minutes
- **Medium term Pin Bars**
  Can be found on 1 hour to 4 hour timeframes
- **Long term Pin Bars**
  Found on daily charts up to Monthly charts

If you find yourself in a trade based off the short term Pin Bar formation:

- Take partial profits and let the remainder of the trade run at break even.
- Or move your stop loss in the money to lock in profits just in case the market moves against you.

Note: Long Term Pin Bars have more significance over short term Pin Bars.

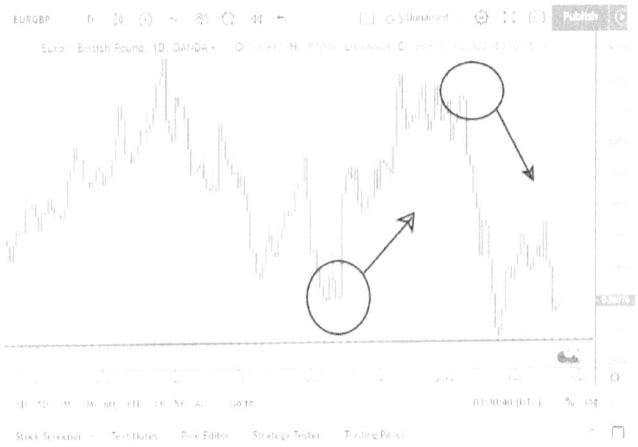

Trade setups taken from Long term Pin Bar formations have a high probability of success which translates to massive pip gains.

Importance of trading long term Pin Bars:

- Less time spent analysing and watching charts for trade setups.
- Trading Long term Pin Bars will allow you to make fewer trades but very high probability trades with a massive win potential.
- Encourages the set and forget trading style, which reduces your emotional interference in your decision making process. You have more free time to yourself and do other personal activities rather than being glued to your computer screen analysing the noisy short term charts.

How many currency pairs do you trade?

I analyse all of them except some exotics, I do not trade most exotics due to their high spreads. I analyse all currency pairs plus a few commodities.

This doesn't mean I trade all these currencies at once. I will place about 1-3 trades a week depending on the available opportunities and this is enough for me to be profitable. I have learnt that it is much profitable to place a few high probability trades than to take allot of emotion filled impulsive trading decisions. Having too many open trades at once can be difficult to successfully manage trades until they fully play out.

Placing a stop loss on daily chart is very large... I can't afford to place an average 30-50 pips stop loss. How does your account survive drawdowns?

The number of pips risked or gained per trade do not really matter. What matters is your overall percentage risk. You can risk less than 10% of your account balance by either setting a risk of 50 pips or 10 pips all you need is to work out your lot size accordingly.

I know you should be asking yourself 'How is that possible?'

This brings us to a very important topic **'Money Management'**. When a trader

 doesn't apply the principles of proper money management to their trading, they are easily parted with their money, accounts are blown and when you see yourself make this facial expression, it might be already too late to save your account. I have been there and have blown enough accounts to actually learn that a good strategy is nothing without proper money management skills.

UNDERTSANDING PROPER MONEY MANAGEMENT SKILLS:

He who learns how to trade acquires a skill that offers an opportunity to run a scalable nomad business and only he who masters money management will enjoy the fruits of this business.

Risk Management:

In trading we have to believe in something that is not entirely certain, that is why it is very important we apply proper money management as we are not going to win all of our trades.

Having experience in educating traders and helping them build their strategies. I strongly recommend that a trader must not risk more than 10% of their account balance on any given trade.

In my position sizing tutorial I teach my clients two types of money management methods that they can apply to their trading.

We will cover this two methods shortly…

(a)Position Sizing:

This is the relationship between the size of your trade in standard lots and the total number of pips risked per trade. This will then determine your overall risk per trade. In order to calculate the position size we need to identify the number of pips we wish to risk per trade and the percentage of the balance we wish to risk-which must not be more than 10% of the total account balance.

Working out a trading position size:

Position size = (Balance*Risk percentage)*(number of pips in decimal points)

Let's take a look at an example on the next page…

John is a Price Action trader, trading an account with a total balance of US$1000. John notices a bullish Pin Bar setup on the daily chart with enough confluence on the GBPUSD pair. John would like to place a buy trade with a risk of 40 pips.

Choosing to risk only 3% of his account. What will be John's position size in standard lots?

We will now use the given equation to calculate John's Position Size...

Pos. size = ($1000*3%) X (0.004pips)

    =0.12 Standard Lots

So given the above scenario John can only buy 12 000 units of the GBUSD pair to risk 3% of his account balance.

Does this make sense? I mean do you understand how to calculate a position size now?

You can have a different stop loss small or big. If you choose to keep your risk constant you can always use this equation to work out your position size.

- With a varying stop loss distance you can still keep your overall risk per trade constant by calculating the position size of your trade.
- Pip value varies from pair to pair, using the position sizing equation we are applying the average value of a micro pip equating to US$1

TWO TYPES OF MONEY MANAGEMENT METHODS:

i. ## Calculate each position

Using the position sizing tutorial on page 46 you can calculate each position size, giving you an approximate standard lot size. You will then apply to meet your required risk appetite per trade. If you hate dealing with equations and doing calculations. You can apply the second method below which is:

ii. ## Using a consistent lot size

In order to apply this method effectively you will need to work out your consistent trade size. To do this you will need to collect data of your previous trades and take an average of your stop loss distance on at least five trades you have previously placed.

Let's say for instance your previous stops are as follows: **50 pips; 30 pips; 40 pips; 20 pips and 50 pips** respectively your average pip value will be 38 pips. So assuming you would like to risk 4% percent of your initial account balance of US$1000.

This will be your consistent lot size amount (using the same position sizing tutorial):

Lot size = ($1000*4%) (0.0038pips)

= 0.152 STD Lots or 15 200

You will then need to calculate a new position size as your account grows in order to compound your account.

Which money management method do you use to trade the market?

Applying the second method reduces the market's psychological pressure and trade size remains the same regardless of the short term account performance.

When trading with this strategy do you consider the news?

The implications of the news releases on price action are all seen within the technical analysis of a chart. The news outbreak does not change the overall trend condition of a currency pair. Therefore, I believe if you are going to trade price action focus on price action only.

TRADING PIN BARS

Trade entry rules:

When trading Pin Bars, I often look for trade setups on the daily timeframe. This is a good way to trade the market, you have less chart time and it also allows you to apply the set and forget trading approach. It is best to try and spot Pin Bar formations at the end of the trading day, and if you find any entries find a profit target and set your stop loss and sit back letting the market do its job.

Why trade the daily chart?

Number 1: Trading signals that appear on the daily chart carry more weight and have a high winning probability.

Number 2: Trades taken from the daily chart will mean a much higher profit target.

Taking much longer to play out but in the end you will find yourself catching pips in the regions of 50-400 pips.

Number 3: Less chart time, meaning you don't have to sit down all day watching your charts trying to find new opportunities. Simply look at your charts at the close of the day and try finding Pin Bar Formations to trade.

Type of Entry:

I often use the instant execution market order type. This is an aggressive entry technique.

HOW TO TRADE PIN BARS:

BUY ENTRY RULES:

A. Identify a Pin Bar and note the supporting factors behind the pin bar formation. The above pin bar formed close to a horizontal support level (area where our stop loss was placed)

B. Set the stop loss just below the low of the pin bar formation.

C. Buy before price action moves above the high of the pin bar. *Buying while the price is within the Low and high area of the pin bar will ensure your stop is not too wide off.*

D. Set profit target at the next horizontal resistance level or keep trailing your stop loss until you get stopped out.

SELL ENTRY RULES:

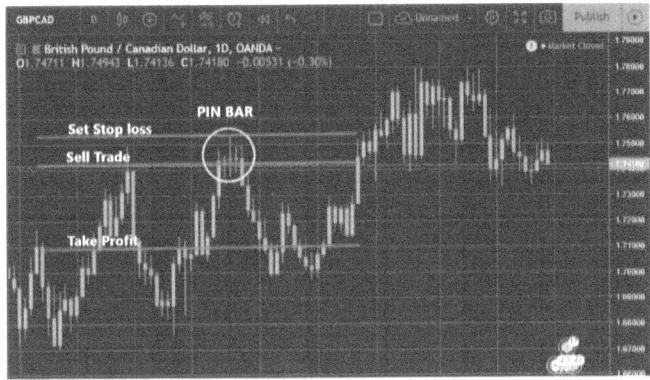

A. Identify a bearish Pin Bar circled area. Notice the double Pin Bar formation? That's the type of Pin Bar we chose to trade. The Pin Bar formed at the horizontal resistance level.

B. Set a stop loss above the high of the pin bar formation.

C. Place a sell trade while price is still within the Low and high price range of the bearish Pin Bar formation.

D. Set take profit at the next horizontal support for a sell trade or keep trailing your stop until the market reverses and stops you out.

Aren't you confusing us by giving us two methods of taking profits? One for setting a profit target and the other for trailing the stop.

No, I am not confusing you at all. I am giving you my experience and you can use either methods for different reasons. Setting a profit target will ensure that your trade will be closed automatically once the market price reaches the set profit target and trailing your stop means you will have to move your stop loss behind support or resistance levels as the market ebbs and flows.

Do I just have to set my trade and forget about it until my profit target is reached?

Once you open a trade you will have to manage your open position well until it reaches your profit target. Let's get into it...

TRADE MANAGEMENT:

There is a cliché that "Opening a trade is very easy, but it is much more challenging to manage an open trade until its full pay-out potential".

Managing an open trade is one thing you need to experience by practicing with paper money before you trade with real money. In most cases where I haven't managed my positions well, I found out that the market reversed against me- having a good trade turn bad because I watched it for too long without taking profits or trailing the stop.

How do you manage an open trade well until its full pay-out potential?

Understand where to properly set your stop loss to avoid being stopped out from the market. When setting a stop loss;

Place your stop below a support level for a buy trade and above a resistance level for a sell trade.

When trading you will need to move your stop loss only when the market test a noticeable support or resistance zone and when these zones hold then move your stop below or above that area.

Mistakes to avoid:

Do not anticipate a support or resistance level. Do not decide whether a level is going to hold or break before the market tests that level.

Some levels are noticeable before they even occur but it's not your job to predict what the market will do next but to follow and obey the footprints of the market.

Let's look at some trade examples on the following page…

MANAGING A BUY TRADE:

Looking at the EURGBP chart below, let's assume that on this particular day a Pin Bar formed on the daily chart. And following the buy entry rules you opened a buy trade.

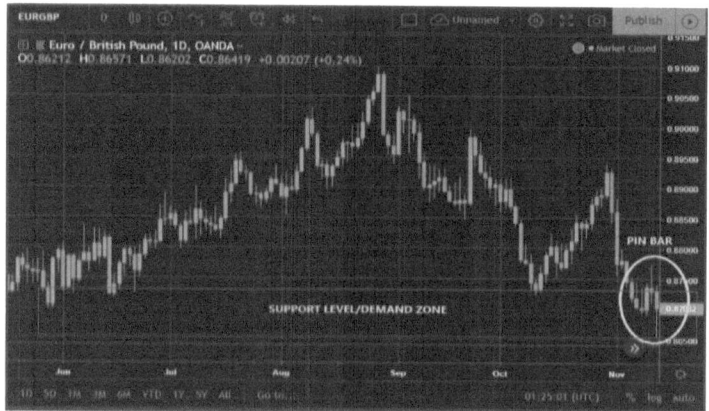

Now let's look at what happens 2 days later.

See how the low of the next candlestick comes close but doesn't reach the stop loss area below the Pin Bar, before the market shoots up the next day heading for the supply zone?

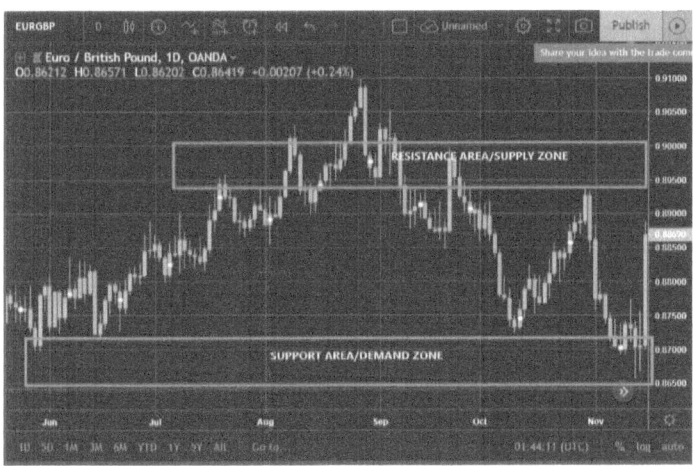

This buy trade didn't take a whole lot of effort to manage just four days into this trade and price has already reached take profit area (at the resistance area) yielding plus 200 pips profit.

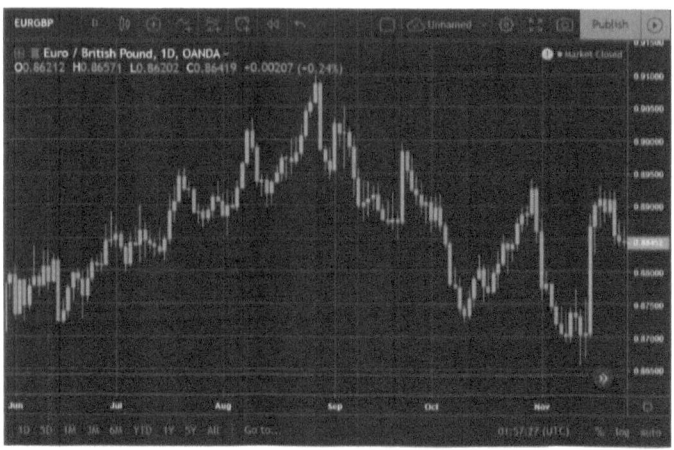

With this trade setup you wouldn't even need to move your stop loss. There are no noticeable support/resistance zones that formed.

MANAGING A SELL TRADE:

Looking at the USDZAR chart below. A Pin Bar formed at a resistance level, most traders will anticipate for a breakout, but as contrarian trader you need to do what most traders won't do. Which is fade the breakout.

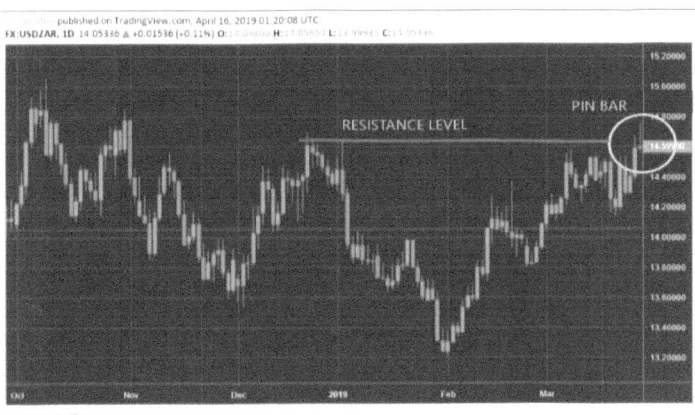

You have just traded the bearish Pin Bar above following the given Sell entry rules.

This is what happens next after 2 days...
Just within two days and you reached
Take profit at the next support level…
Easy right? Just a little practice will do,

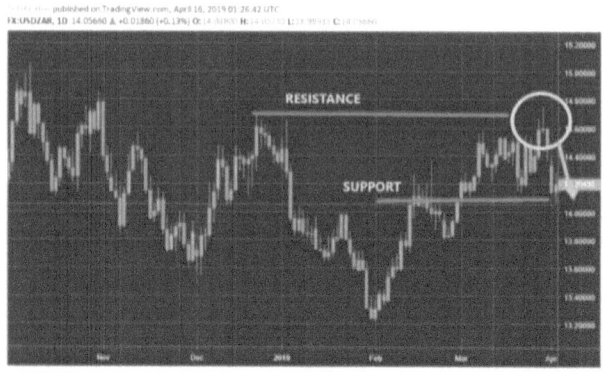

WHEN TRADING PIN BARS YOU WILL
REALISE THAT ONCE A PIN BAR FORMS
ON YOUR CHART. YOU MIGHT START TO
DOUBT AND ASK YOURSELF ALL
QUESTIONS THAT MIGHT MAKE YOU NOT
TO TAKE THE TRADE. BUT YOU KNOW
WHAT? THAT'S NORMAL. IF YOU SEE A
PIN BAR WITH ENOUGH CONFLUENCE TO
IT. TRADE IT!

Let us now take a look at this chart below… Do you remember this chart from the first page? Right, this is one of my best Bearish Pin Bar trades.

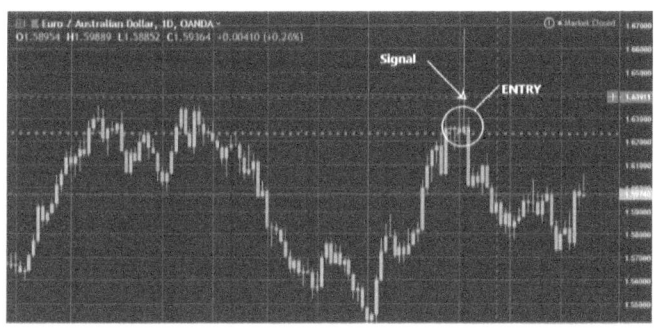

A clear long tailed Pin Bar just formed on the EURAUD chart and it really stood out, there was no way any price action trader would have missed this trade.

Following the entry rules for a sell trade I opened a sell trade and within just a couple of hours I was able to move my stop loss to break even, meaning my risk on this trade was reduced to zero.

Moving your stop loss to break-even means you have an opportunity to even increase your position size and capitalize on a single trade.Let us zoom in on the four hour chart below... This is what was happening about 10 hours later into this trade.

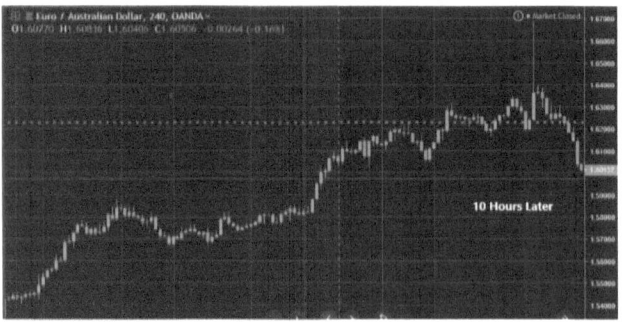

The reasons why I like trading daily pin bars are:

Number 1: You do not need to analyse charts all day

Number 2: You don't need to apply indicators to your charts and learn all the meanings of these indicators.

Number 3: I set my trade and forget about it and check on it the next day or so.

Number 4: When a Pin Bar is traded with enough supporting factor your winning probability increases.

When I speak of supporting factors or confluence I am talking about:

- Support and Resistance level (both horizontal and diagonal)
- The overall trend of the price

Once these above factors are well aligned with a pin bar formation, you have a high probability trade in the making.

For example: A bullish pin bar forming near a support level while price is trending upwards will mean a high probability buy trade.

Don't take my word for it let me show
you some charts to prove this…

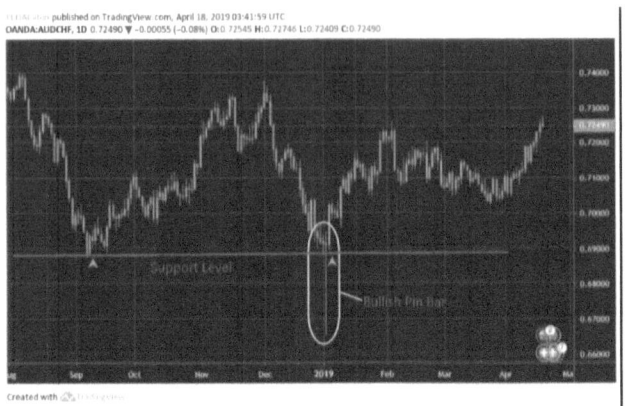

Take a look at the AUDCHF daily chart
above. A bullish Pin Bar formed on the
daily chart, if you look at the left hand
side of the chart, the body of the pin bar
formed adjacent to the previous low
(indicated with blue arrow on the left).
This together signifies a support level
which we regard as confluence or a
supporting factor that price is most likely
to surge in the upwards direction.

Look at what happens on the following day above… A strong bullish candlestick forms making this a good buy trade. With this trade you could have easily scored over 200 pips within a five day period. Patients is everything in this game.

Let us look at another chart example in real life, so that you get a clearer outlook…Looking at the daily AUDUSD chart below, a bullish Pin Bar formed at an event area or rather say a support level.

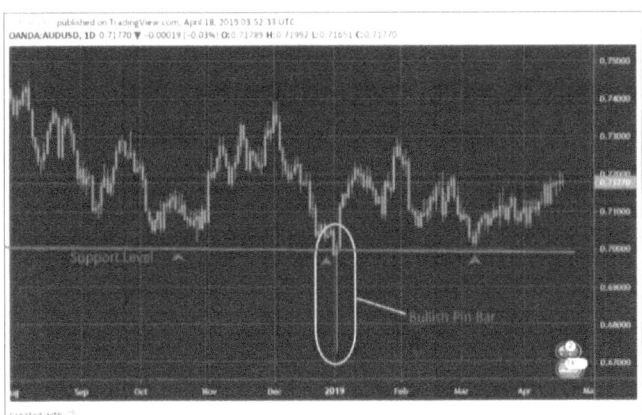

We see as the long tailed Bullish Pin Bar makes a clear print on the chart. On the left hand side is a previous trough or swing low making this a support area.

What does it mean to you when price actions makes not only a pin bar but also forms a pin bar at support or resistance level? We call this an additional factor known as confluence or supporting factor.

Right? This is what even adds more weight to our bias. So that you are not stuck looking at your charts not knowing if it is the right time to pull a trigger or not (the dear in the headlights notion). But with enough supporting factors it's quite easy to pull the trigger.

So you mean we must only trade Pin Bars that occur at event areas or areas of support and resistance?

Pin Bars form almost everywhere on the chart. But the ones that form at event areas have a higher probability of defining the market direction. So if you want to be on the higher probability side of winning trades. Trade pin bars that form with enough confluence behind them.

Let us take a final look at the daily NZDJPY chart below…

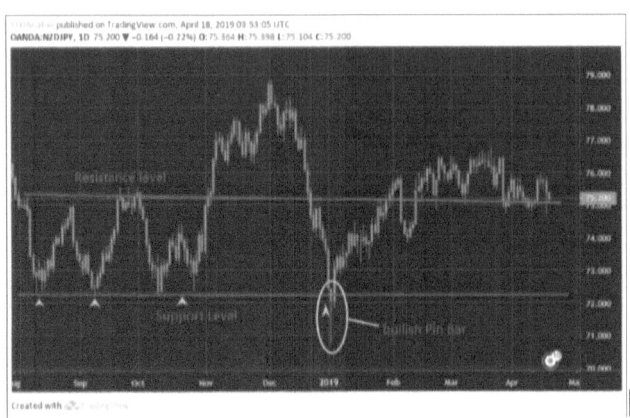

et us summarise the few factors that will lead to opening a buy trade by looking at the above chart:

- Bullish Pin Bar formation at circled area
- Supporting factor- Bullish Pin Bar forms at a support level. Looking on the left hand side these level was tested several times before the bullish Pin Bar Formed.

- Once you open a trade always place your profit target at the next resistance level.

Now you have to do your homework. Look at your charts and find the same pin bar formations and see if you can also identify supporting factors for your findings. Also note down if it would have been successful taking those trades…Take out a pen and start by analysing the daily USDJPY chart below.

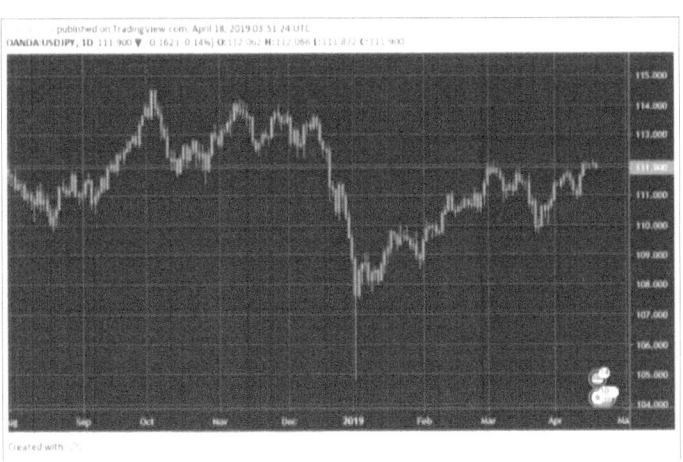

What are your findings?

NOW THAT YOU HAVE LEANRT HOW TO TRADE PRICE ACTION BY ANALYSING PIN BARS… IT IS TIME TO APPLY WHAT YOU HAVE LEARNT FROM THIS BOOK AND PUT IT TO WORK!

REMEMBER, this might seem like an easy thing to do but it is not.

YOUR EMOTIONS WILL BE RIGHT THERE AND MIGHT CAUSE YOU TO BACK SLIDE ON SOME OPPORTUNITIES. TAKE UP EVERY OPPORTUNITY WITH CONFIDENCE. YOU WON"T WIN ALL YOUR TRADES BUT IF YOU REMAIN CONSITENT YOU WILL HAVE A PROFITABLE RECORD.

BUY WHEN IT SAYS BUY AND SELL WHEN IT SAYS SELL. DON'T OVER ANALYSE JUST TRADE AND WALK AWAY.

FOREX DIALOGUE

I would like to congratulate you for taking time to complete the first section of P.A.U.I

However, if you have read the first chapter and could not just digest most of the content or you felt the terms used were extra ordinary. You might be new to FOREX trading and…

…I dedicate this section of Price Action the Ultimate Indicator to beginners in the FOREX Market and I would also advise you to do further research to compound your knowledge regarding the financial markets.

Join me as I take you through the basics of trading in my FOREX DIALOGUE

BROKERS

In order to trade the FOREX Market you will need to pick a broker to trade with. There are a lot of brokers to choose from. But here are a few bits of information to help you pick a broker.

- **Spread**

   This is the difference between the asking and bidding price of a currency at which it can be bought and sold at a given time. Usually calculated in pips this is the way brokers make money as they do not charge any commission. Spreads differ from broker to broker and choosing a broker with a low spread is the best choice you can make.

- **Regulated Broker**

  Make sure your broker is regulated by the financial body within the region it operates in. This information is available on the broker's website
- **Account Type**

  Choosing the account type to trade with is very important. Most brokers offer the ECN and STP types of accounts. ECN accounts being a good choice for less experienced traders as you can start off with a little investment meaning your exposure to risk is less and STP accounts are more suitable for experienced traders.

As a trader is your duty to understand your broker well. Join forums to understand the type of broker you are dealing with and also understand the margin rules applied by your broker.

As you trade you are trading with leveraged money in laymen terms borrowed money and your broker can liquidate your position at any time if your trade takes a dive and you do not have enough funds in your account to keep your position open.

CURRENCY QUOTES

Currencies are traded against one another in quotes or pairs. A currency pair is quoted in two ways. Either as a direct quote or an indirect quote. Direct quote is simply a foreign exchange where the foreign currency is the base currency, while an indirect quote is whereby the domestic currency is the base currency

Let's say you are looking at the USD/ZAR currency pair. USD is the base currency while the South African rand (ZAR) is the counter currency. If you are based in South Africa this will be a direct quote. Direct meaning that in order to purchase the USD currency you will have to pay the quoted price on the Foreign Exchange.

Cross Currency

These are currency quotes given without the USD currency as part of the currency pair. Common cross currency pairs are such as the AUDCFH, EURNZD, EURGBP and so forth. Cross currency pairs give the forex trader a large variety of currency pairs to trade.

Spreads and Pips

Looking at major currency pairs such as the USDCAD, EURUSD and GBPUSD, a pip will be equal to 0.0001. However, if you look at currency pairs such as the USDZAR and USDJPY you will notice that these pairs only goes to two decimal places. So one pip will be 0.01.

Although these currency increments may seem very small. Small changes may result in large profits or losses, due to leverage used in the Forex market.

UNDERSTANDING LEVERAGE

Leverage is known as spending power by using borrowed investment capital from your broker. Basically, the more leveraged your account is the more risky your trading position will be. A small increase or decrease in a number of pips might mean big profit or loss on your account. Let's say for instance you trading a standard lot which is $100,000 the approximate pip value of a standard lot is $10 a Pip. If your account has a balance of $1000 and a leverage of 500:1 meaning you have about $500,000 in borrowed investment capital and you can buy a maximum of 5 standard lots at a time.

So it will be entirely risky to trade 5 lots because this means you can blow your account if the markets moves about 20 pips against you and you also stand a chance of doubling your account if the market moves 20 pips in your favour. Leverage is a double sided sword and proper money management should be applied when investing with a highly leveraged account.

LOTS

In forex trading the amount of currency bought or sold is measured as lots- $100,000 is typically a standard lot. There are also smaller lot sizes usually less than $100,000 known as mini lots. These may seem as large numbers but for trade to generate a reasonable amount of profit or loss there should be a great change in number of pips the currency moves. Normally these increments are quite small that is why a large amount of a currency is required to make a reasonable profit.

THE VALUE OF A PIP

How does one calculate the profit and loss of a trading position? Suppose you bought USDJPY. The USD is the base currency and JPY is the quote currency. You bought USDJPY when it was at 104.23 and it went up to 104.24 the change in this currency will 0.01 which is one pip. Assuming you bought 1lot ($100,000 units) of USDJPY your profit will be ($100,000X0.01) = 1000 yen. You will then divide this by the current quote price 104.24. The profit in dollar amount will be $9.59

FINALLY, I WOULD LIKE TO DEDICATE THIS BOOK TO MY FIRST BORN CHILD. THAT IS WHY I DECIDED TO RELEASE THIS BOOK IN JUNE 2019 (THE MONTH MY CHILD IS BORN). THIS IS MY FIRST BOOK AND I HAVE PUT IN SO MUCH EFFORT TO MAKE SURE IT CREATES A GREAT IMPACT AND CHANGE PEOPLE"S FINANCIAL STATUS AROUND THE WORLD.

IF AND WHEN YOU ARE HAVING GREAT SUCCESS WITH THE PIN BAR TRADING STRATEGY. PLEASE, IT WILL BE A GREAT PLEASURE TO HEAR FROM YOU.

KINDLY SEND ME AN EMAIL
tedacabin@gmail.com